R.E.I. Editions

All our ebooks can be read on the following devices:

- Computer
- eReader
- iOS
- Android
- Blackberry
- Window
- Tablet
- Mobile phone

Brown Kittel

Fieseler Fi 103 - The V-1

ISBN: 9782372975421

Publication: March 2025

www.rei-editions.com

Brown Kittel

Fieseler Fi 103
The V-1

R.E.I. Editions

Index

The V- 1

The Fieseler Fi 103, better known as the V-1, internally designated with the code name FZG 76 (Flakzielgerät - anti-aircraft gun target), was a war device developed by the German company Gerhard-Fieseler-Werke in the early 1940s and used by the Luftwaffe in the final phase of the Second World War.
Gerhard-Fieseler-Werke GmbH, also referred to simply as Fieseler-Werke and Fieseler, was a German aircraft manufacturing company founded in the 1930s by World War I ace and aerobatic pilot Gerhard Fieseler.
The company, based in Kassel, which operated under the name Fieseler Flugzeugbau until 1 April 1939, was active in the development and production of aircraft for the civil general aviation market, as well as military aircraft and weapons systems used by the Luftwaffe during the Second World War, including the single-engine STOL Fieseler Fi 156 "Storch" and the self-propelled flying bomb Fieseler Fi 103, better known as the V-1.
The V-1, the acronym stands for Vergeltungswaffen 1, translated from the German “Retaliatory Weapon 1” and thus renamed by Joseph Goebbels for propaganda purposes, combined the characteristics of an airplane with those of an aeronautical bomb and can be considered the first example of a cruise missile.
In the autumn of 1936, while working for the Argus aircraft engine company, Fritz Gosslau, building on the experience gained on the Argus As 292 (military designation FZG 43), a small remotely controlled reconnaissance aircraft, began work on the development of a remote aircraft control system.

On November 9, 1939, the company sent a letter to the Reichsluftfahrt ministerium, the ministry responsible at the time. of aviation civil And military from the Germany, a preliminary project for the construction of a remote-controlled aircraft.

On private initiative, Argus, asking for the collaboration of Lorentz and Arado Flugzeugwerke, started a first development with The name Project "Fernfire".

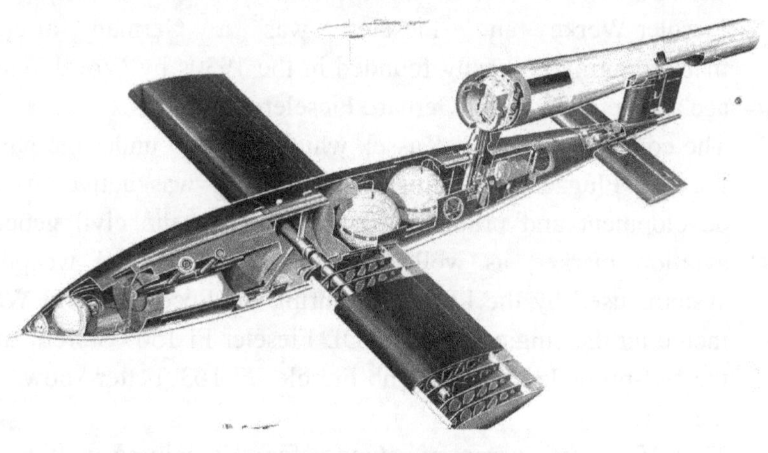

The The aircraft, simply called Lufttorpedo, flying torpedo, was proposed in three variants capable of carrying a war load of 1,000 kg to an operational altitude of 5,000 metres.

- The first ones were to be equipped with a 12-cylinder inverted V Argus As 410 with 500 HP, at a cruising speed of 700 km/h, the last one with a new type of engine , then to the first phases Of development, The pulse jet, a jet engine capable of providing 150 kg of thrust and which would have guaranteed a projected cruising speed of 750 km/h.

A further development, which received the internal designation Project P 35 "Erfurt", was again submitted by Gosslau to the RLM authorities in April 1940 , but on 31 May Rudolf Bree replied that he saw no possible use for such a solution and that remote control of the device was a further weakness of the project.

On January 6, 1941, Heinrich Koppenberg, the director of Argus, in an attempt to save the project, obtained a meeting with Ernst Udet to try to convince him to continue its development, but Udet announced his decision to cancel it. Nonetheless, Gosslau was convinced that the basic idea was sound and began work again to simplify the project.

Rear view of the V-1 at IWM Duxford, showing section of the launch pad.

Since Argus, being an engine manufacturer, lacked the capacity to produce a fuselage for the project, Koppenberg asked Robert Lusser, chief designer and head of the technical department at Heinkel, to assist him in the development phases. On 27

February 1942, Lusser, who had moved to Gerhard-Fieseler-Werke on 22 January, managed to meet with Koppenberg and acquire the details of the project Of Goslau. Lusser no modified further the configuration by abandoning the proposed solution with two pulsejet engines for a single engine.
The final development of the project was presented to the RLM Technical Office on 5 June, where it was approved, given the official designation Fi 103, and Fieseler was assigned the task of supplying the prototype for evaluation. On 19 June, Generalfeldmarschall Erhard Milch gave the Fi 103 top priority for series production as soon as possible, and the development program was transferred to the Luftwaffe test center at Karlshagen.

- The V-1 was developed in the base secret Of Peenemunde, located to approximately 230 km from Berlin, on the shores of the Baltic Sea.

This gigantic centre, built in 1937, included a large number of laboratories and an immense production centre:
Next to it, a town had been built for the engineers, the staff and their families: this centre, under the direction of Walter Dornberger and Wernher Von Braun, employed more than 12,000 people and was the most modern in the world at the beginning of the Second World War.
On 30 August Fiesler completed the first airframe and the first Fi 103 prototype took flight on 10 December 1942, when it was released from a Focke-Wulf Fw 200 specially equipped for gliding flight.

- The V-1s were designed to be as inexpensive and simple as possible.

Each one cost 3,500 Marks, which was 1/10 of the price of a V-2 rocket.
The first flight came carried out on 23 December 1942 with a

launch from a ramp: the prototype travelled a distance of only 3 km. Numerous developments were made and it can be said that the device was finally perfected on 26 June 1943 with the launch of prototype number 65 which travelled a distance of 234 km.

- The launch velocity was actually around 402 km/h (250 mph), which created up to 17 g at launch.

Beginning in January 1941, the V-1's jet engine was also tested on a variety of craft, including an experimental attack boat known as the Tornado, in which a boat loaded with a 700 kg (1,543 lb) warhead was directed toward a target ship by remote control or by a pilot jumping out of the back at the last moment. The development, testing and use of the V-1 in the Third Reich were top secret: between 19 and 29 March 1945, orders were issued by the Führer to destroy all production and research documents.

Technique

Thc V-1 was designed under the code name Kirschkern from Lusser and Goslau, with a fuselage constructed mainly of welded steel plates and wings fabricated using the same technique, or in plywood.
The simple pulsejet operated at about 50 pulses per second and the distinctive buzz it produced earned the device the nickname "buzz."

- The flying bomb used an Argus As 014 pulse jet engine.

This type of aircraft engine could not be used effectively for manned warplanes, as it was difficult to start, inefficient above 3,000 meters, of short duration and practically unable to change speed.
All these characteristics were, instead, largely compatible with a flying bomb, which could, instead, take advantage of the great construction simplicity of this type of engine, combined with speed performances of absolute importance for the time.
The characteristic large vibrations produced by the pulsejets led to the external and rear installation of the Argus.

- No were produced about 31,100 copies.

It provided a thrust of 272 kg corresponding to about 700 hp at cruising speed. In the first model, tested on 13 November 1939, the air entered the engine from the rear and was accelerated by a device called a blower of Borda who also provided for the compression and recirculation of the air and fuel mixture in the chamber combustion to then be expelled from the exhaust nozzle, consisting of a duct coaxial to the inlet one.
This configuration was soon discarded due to irregular combustion.

The second model featured a frontal entry of pressurized air in a room Of combustion spherical Where was deflected giving rise to an annular vortex.

- From the third model onwards the Borda's mouth, and the resulting ring vortex, by applying a reed valve at the inlet developed by the German scientist Paul Schmidt.

The first engine was tested in flight on 28 April 1941, installed on a specially modified Gotha Go 145 biplane. In the summer of 1942 a pair of engines was installed on a DFS 230-A1 transport glider, which, after being state towed in share And unhooked, there lit up And became the first airplane to the world to fly pushed from pulse jets, although the engines caused considerable damage to the glider's structure.
It was also tested on the Messerschmitt Bf 110 in an attempt to increase its maximum speed, but experiments on aircraft were soon abandoned to concentrate efforts on the V-1 flying bombs.

- In August 1944, the final modification was made to the fuel control system, which allowed the V-1 to reach a speed of 765 km/h.

In its final version, the engine consisted of a sheet of metal bent into a tube; at the front were a series of spring-controlled reed valves, a fuel injection system and a spark plug.
To start the engine, a plug was placed in the nozzle to saturate the combustion chamber with acetylene: at the same time, when the spark plug ignited, a portable source of compressed air provided the oxygen necessary for starting for the time needed for the operating temperature to stabilize.

- At that point the electrical and pneumatic power was removed and the combustion continued on its own.

Each cycle, or pulse, of the engine began with the valves open. Fuel injected downstream was ignited and the resulting expansion of the combustion gases closed the valves, but the subsequent drop in pressure in the combustion chamber due to the expulsion of exhaust gases from the nozzle reopened the valves, new air was flowing and the cycle could thus repeat at a frequency of about 45-55 times per second.

Pulse jet Argus As 014 installed on a split Of V- 1.

The electric ignition system was used only at start-up: at full speed, it was the backfire in the nozzle to ensure the ignition of the fresh mixture.
The fuel tank, typically petrol, was placed pressurized by compressed air also used by the automatic guidance system. The fuel control system continuously supplied fuel to the injectors at a pressure that varied depending on the flight conditions.
Unlike other pulsejets of the time, which used a structured air intake shut-off valve as the petals Of a flower, the Argus employee For The V-1 used a metal grid created with spacers.

Along the openings of the grille, small rectangular slats were mounted, riveted on one side and free to vibrate on the other, so as to close or open the gaps for incoming air, depending on whether the prevailing pressure from the inside, due to the deflagration in the combustion chamber, or the aerodynamic pressure produced by the air.

- In the V-1 The cycle Yes he repeated 47 times per second.

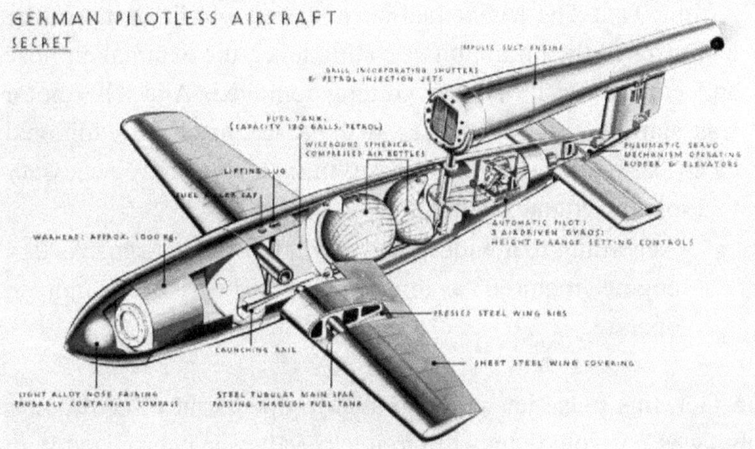

This metal slat system was simple to construct and did not require skilled labor or sophisticated machinery, features that were appreciated in wartime.

The combustion chamber was located 76 centimetres behind the air intake grille, in which the initial ignition was controlled by a spark plug derived from the automotive industry, powered by an autonomous electrical unit which was then disconnected at the moment of launch.

- The fuel, common low-octane gasoline, was injected directly using the pressure of the compressed air reserve also used to keep the steering gyroscopes rotating and to move the control surfaces.

Three air nozzles at the front of the pulse jet They were connected to an external source of compressed air, which was used to start the engine.

- Acetylene gas was usually used for ignition, and very often a wooden panel (or similar) was placed at the end of the exhaust pipe to prevent fuel from escaping. Before of the ignition.

A time That The engine had been started and the temperature had reached the minimum operating level, the external air hose and connectors they were coming removed, And The motor was starting to "fire" pulses without the need for additional electrical ignition systems: these, in fact, were only necessary to allow the engine to start.

- According to a widespread myth, the V-1's Argus As 014 engine required a minimum speed of 240 km/h to operate.

In fact, this pulse jet was also able to operate at a fixed point: this was possible thanks to the intake valves synchronized with the ignition of the mixture in the combustion chamber.
Archive footage from that period clearly shows the distinctive pulsating exhaust of the engine at full throttle, running before from the departure of the weapon from the launch catapult.

- The origin of this myth is probably due to the fact that the static thrust of the pulse jet is rather low And there speed Of stall from the small wings Very tall, there The V-1 would not have been capable of taking off on its own over short distances, and would therefore require either an aircraft catapult, or an airdrop from a modified bomber, such as a Heinkel He 111.

The V1 in launch position, as reconstructed at the Imperial War Museum, Duxford.

The V-1 was usually launched from a sloped launch pad using an apparatus known as a Dampferzeuger ("steam generator") that used hydrogen peroxide and permanganate. of potassium (T-Stoff and Z-Stoff).

- The take off it happened at the speed Of 580 km/h.

Beginning in January 1941, the V-1 pulse jet was tested on a variety of vehicles, including automobiles and an experimental attack craft known as the of Tornado.
This unsuccessful vessel was a variant of a Sprengboot: according to the designers, this vessel, loaded with explosives, was to be guided towards a target ship by a pilot, who was to abandon the vessel at the last moment.

The Tornado came assembled using some hulls Of seaplane connected to a catamaran, with a small cockpit on the connecting beams.
The Tornado prototype was deemed noisy and had disappointing performance, and was therefore abandoned in favour of smaller craft. more conventional, propulsion from normal piston engines.

The pulse reactor

The pulse jet, or pulsereactor, is a very simple form of an exo-reactor in which combustion occurs intermittently providing a pulsed thrust.

Unlike the ramjet (the jet engine it most closely resembles), it is capable of providing thrust at a fixed point (i.e. at zero flight speed).

The first studies on the pulse jet date back to the beginning of the 20th century, when Victor De Karavodine in France patented, the 10 April of the 1907, The first model of pulse jet.

In 1910 a patent was also granted to the engineer Belgian Georges Marconet, but Both solutions remained at the stage of laboratory models.

With the end of the First World War, military interest in this type of engine also began to wane.

In 1939 the Reich Air Ministry decided to promote jet engine research and awarded each car manufacturer has a different technological solution to develop.

- Argus was awarded the pulse jet, the As 014 model designed by the German engineer Fritz Gosslau, will find there its Before application practice on the V- 1.

Used almost exclusively by the V-1 flying bomb (Fieseler Fi 103), it holds the record for being the first engine of its kind to be mass-produced.

- Approximately 31,100 examples were produced.

Later, some pulse jets mounted on the rockets were used, but always remaining within the experimental field. on helicopters. In this case the engines were placed at the ends of the rotor blades. Mounted according to this scheme, the pulsejets had the great advantage of not producing the characteristic torque, thus allowing the creation of aircraft more simple unprovided Of rotor Of tail and related transmission systems.

- Pulse jets are characterized by extreme simplicity and low production costs.

The main drawback is their high noise level and high fuel consumption, which limits their application range. application to the uses military And to few other applications. Today the greatest use of pulsejets is in dynamic aeronautical modelling.

Like many jet engines, the pulsejet is an internal combustion engine of very simple design, consisting essentially of a long tube into which air enters, is mixed with fuel to create a combustible mixture. The difference that distinguishes pulsejets from other engines, such as turbojets or ramjets, is that the combustion that occurs inside the engine is not a continuous process but occurs in the form of repeated explosions, pulses, from which the name of the engine itself derives.

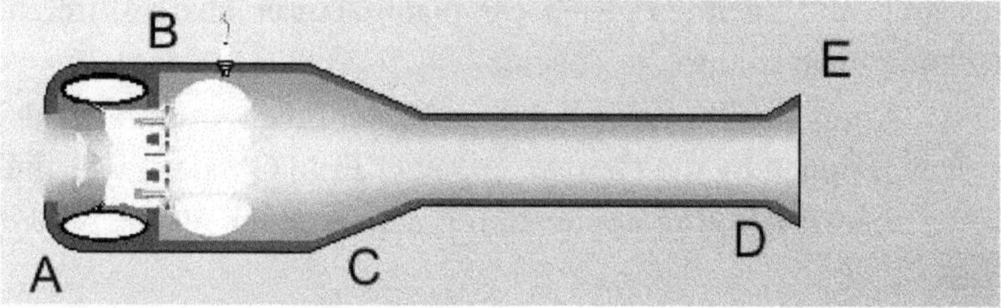

A) aspiration And injection of the fuel
B) valves
C) room Of combustion
D) nozzle
E) expelled gases

In practice, the pulse jet works with external air entering from the front, where the valve is located or not, this is mixed with

the fuel which is injected into the combustion chamber.
Here the mixture is ignited and finally the burnt gases exit from the rear thus producing thrust.
The first ignition must be done by introducing compressed air, with a compressor or an air cylinder, into the engine or more simply by forcing it inside via the air intake.

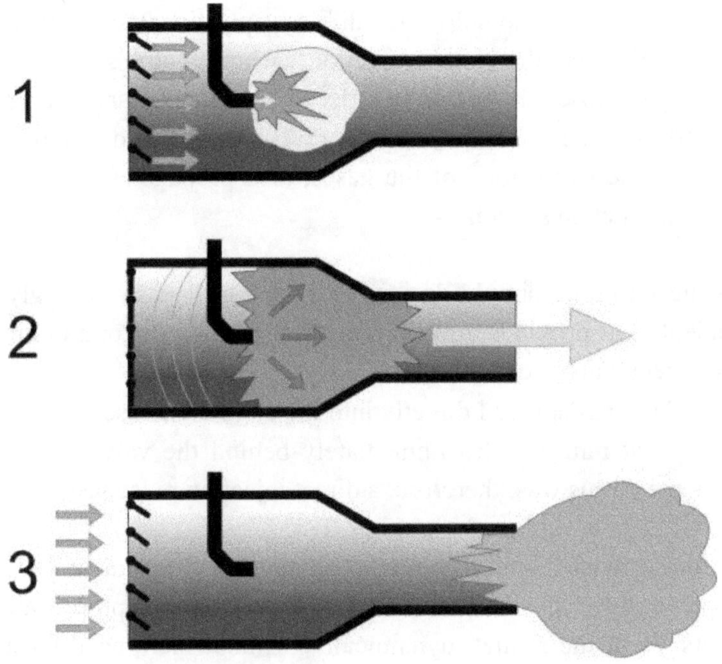

Scheme of the pulse reactor with valve:

- In the first image, the injected fuel it is mixed with the air entering from the left end and, through a suitable initial ignition system (during normal operation it is generally possible to exploit the backfire for ignition), the combustion of the mixture created is triggered.

- In figure number two, the developed combustion

generates pressure waves that propagate throughout the entire system, and, as a consequence of the expansion due to combustion, the gases escape from the right end, an expulsion that generates a depression in the suction section of the system that allows the air to be drawn in for the next cycle (figure three).

- The figure also shows (in different positions) some reed valves in the intake section, whose purpose is to open/close this section in order to allow the passage of air during the intake phase and prevent the thrust developed by the expulsion. of the gases, also propagates through the suction section.

Despite its rather simple design, the valve grill is surprisingly efficient as it provides a much straighter path for incoming air than a petal valve configuration.

- Fuel was sprayed directly into the engine via a series (3 x 3) of nine nozzles immediately behind the valve grille: the Argus was, therefore, a direct injection pulse jet.

The pulse reactor And a motor to combustion internal of very simple design, in which the compression of the captured air occurs, as in the ramjet, dynamically, without there need Of a compressor; unlike of the in other exo-reactors combustion does not occur according to a continuous, but pulsed process . The incoming air is mixed with the fuel in the combustion chamber.

- The ignition of the mixture can be controlled by a spark plug (typically at start-up) or caused by the return flame of the previous combustion phase (at full speed).

The resulting increase in pressure causes acceleration and expulsion of the gases burned by the exhaust nozzle, thus providing thrust.

Backflow through the air intake is prevented by mechanical or "aerodynamic" valves (in valveless engines).

- The next depression That Yes he comes to have in room Of combustion recalls new air and the cycle can Like this to repeat itself Between the 40 and 250 times per second, depending on the type and size of the motor.

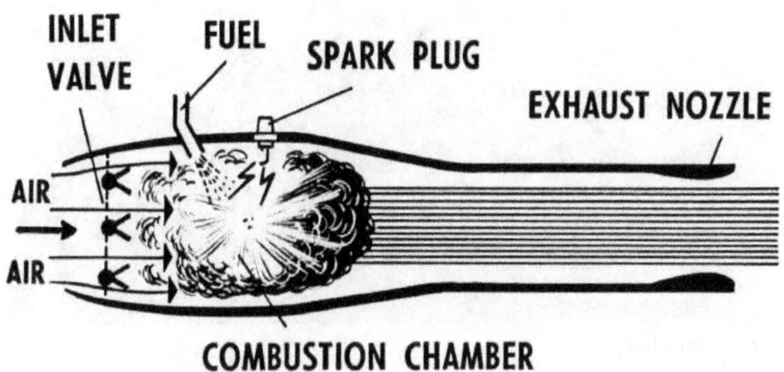

A from the peculiarity of the pulse reactor And that of being able to self-feed, that is, to spontaneously aspirate combustion air thanks to the depression that is generated in the front section of the device, a characteristic that makes the pulse jet capable of providing thrust even at a fixed point (at zero speed), once turned on.

Basically they exist two types of pulse jet:

- **Pulse jet with valves**

In this configuration, the flow of gases inside the engine is partially controlled by a system of reed valves which, acting as a check valve, allows the passage of gases in one direction only. The Achilles heel of this solution is its fragility. of the slats which limits the engine operating life of a few hours of continuous operation.

Valve lamellar.

- **Pulse jet without valves**

The first pulse jet models were built without valves (valveless), but, using particular geometric configurations (such as, for example, the Borda mouth), an attempt was made to create vortical flows with the dual purpose of mixing the incoming air with the fuel and increasing the pressure of the mixture by confining it in the combustion chamber.
These early configurations, however, were particularly inefficient due to losses of fresh mixture expelled from the air intake and total pressure losses due to induced turbulence.
Between the late 1940s and the mid 1950s In the fifties, attempts were made to study "aerodynamic valves" which, by "tuning" the geometry of the air intake and the nozzle with the resonance of the pressure waves, allowed for smooth operation and with efficiencies equal to those of engines with reed valves. Among these, the engines "Escopette" and "He lived" from the

French SNECMA or the AS-11 installed on the Dutch Aviolanda AT-21 drone.

- There The total lack of moving parts in these configurations allows for advantages in terms of reliability and low construction costs.

A development of the pulsejet, which is still being pursued today, is the Pulse Detonation Engine or PDE.

This engine works very similarly to a traditional pulse jet but generates its propulsive force through the detonation and not the deflagration of the air/fuel mixture. This new type of engine promises comparable (if not superior) efficiencies to turbofans, especially at high flight speeds.

- The first flight of an aircraft powered by a Pulse Detonation Engine took place at the Mojave Air & Space Port on January 31, 2008.

The main difference between a PDE and a traditional pulse jet is that the mixture in the combustion chamber does not undergo subsonic combustion, but is brought to complete a detonation supersonic.

- In the PDE, Oxygen and fuel combine to create gases that move at supersonic speeds (essentially an explosion rather than combustion).
- The other difference is that the shut-off valves are replaced by devices more sophisticated, too if in some projects Of General Electric's PDE, any locking device is eliminated thanks to a careful choice of timing, using the differences Of pressure Between the different areas of the motor, to the to ensure that hot gases are expelled backwards.

Specifications techniques

- Length: 3.66 meters
- Diameter maximum: 588mm
- Diameter tube Of exhaust: 380mm
- Length from exhaust: 1.75 meters
- Weight: 153 kg
- Push static: 500 pounds
- Push max: 800 pounds
- Consumption of fuel: 3.4kg / lb / hr

Thermodynamic cycle analysis

The operation of the pulse jet is based fundamentally on the Venturi effect, more precisely in conjunction with the area Of minor section from the room Of combustion.
The thermal cycle described is called Lenoir cycle and is characterized by the total absence of the compression process, which determines a thermodynamic efficiency much lower than the classic Otto and Diesel cycles.

Phase Of combustion (1- 2)

Point 1 represents the initial condition of the fluid (air-fuel mixture) that fills the combustion chamber. The heat introduction q1 referred to the unit of mass, produces isochoric combustion. At this stage the work is zero.

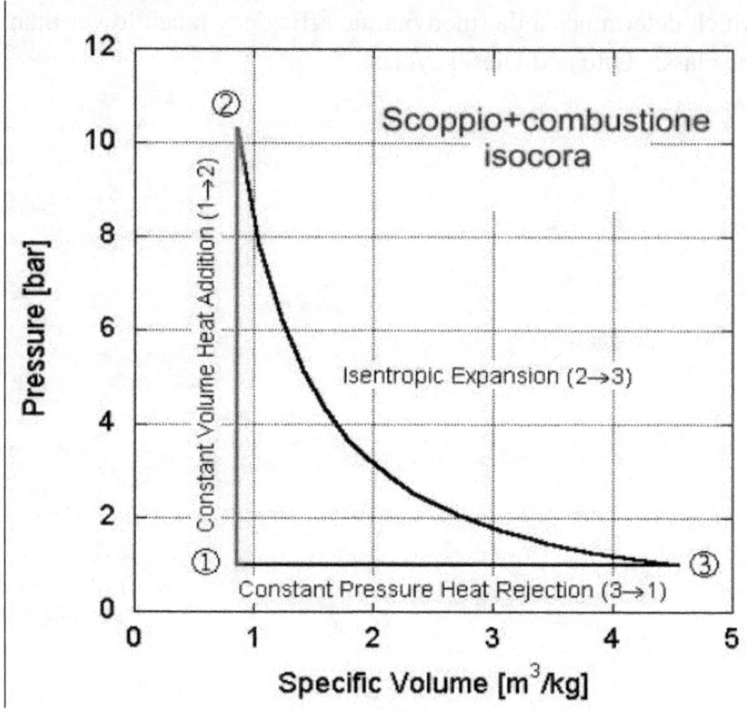

Expansion phase (2-3)

The expansion occurs in a reversible adiabatic manner and returns the fluid to the original pressure.
This is the only active phase of the cycle.
The Work And given from the relation: $L_3 = m*cv (T_2 - T_3)$.

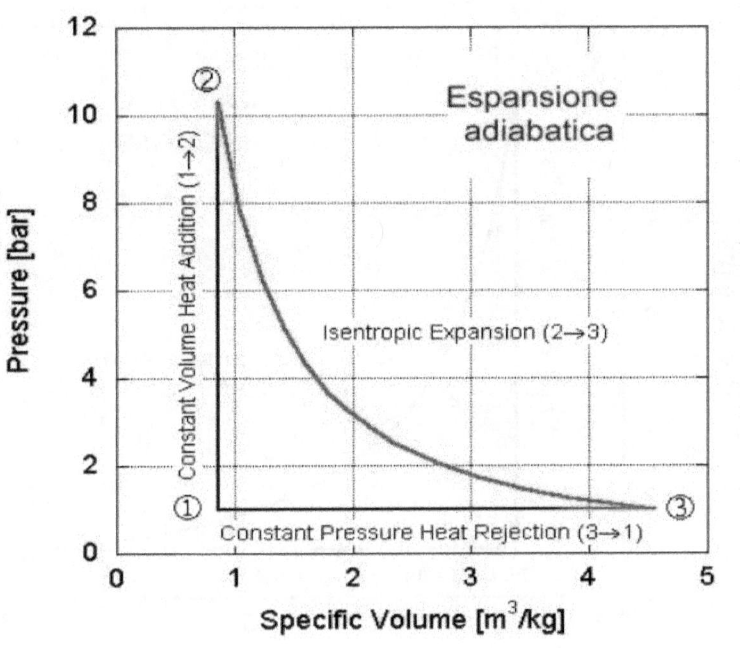

Phase Of I unload (3- 1)

During the discharge phase, the fluid is brought back to its original temperature through constant pressure cooling. At this stage the work is given by the relationship:
$L_4 = p_1 * (V_1 - V_3)$.

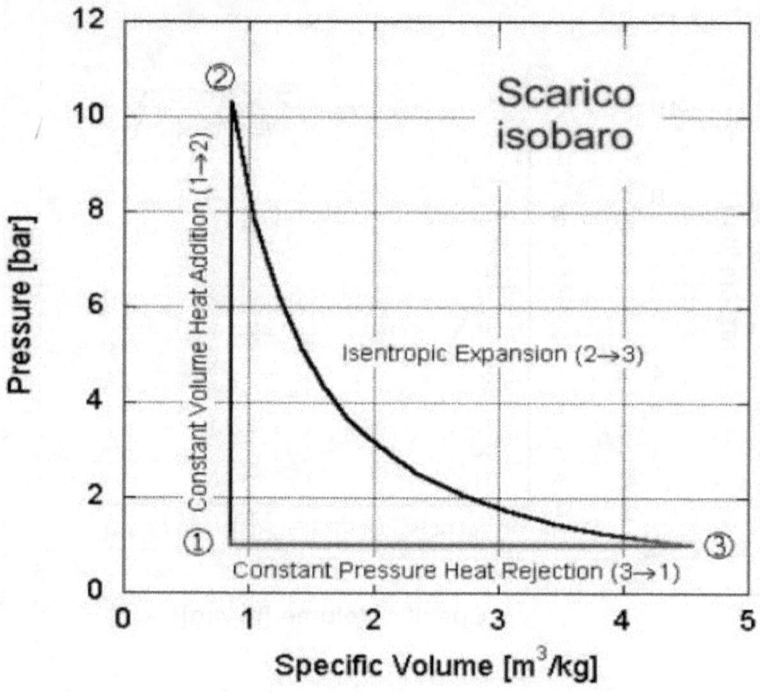

The useful work is represented graphically by the area enclosed by the pV graph and is: $Ltot = L_3 + L_4$.
The yield, on the other hand, is given by the ratio between total work and the heat Q_2 needed to start the combustion and is given by the relation:
$\eta_{total} = L_{total} / m * c_v * (T_2 - T_1)$

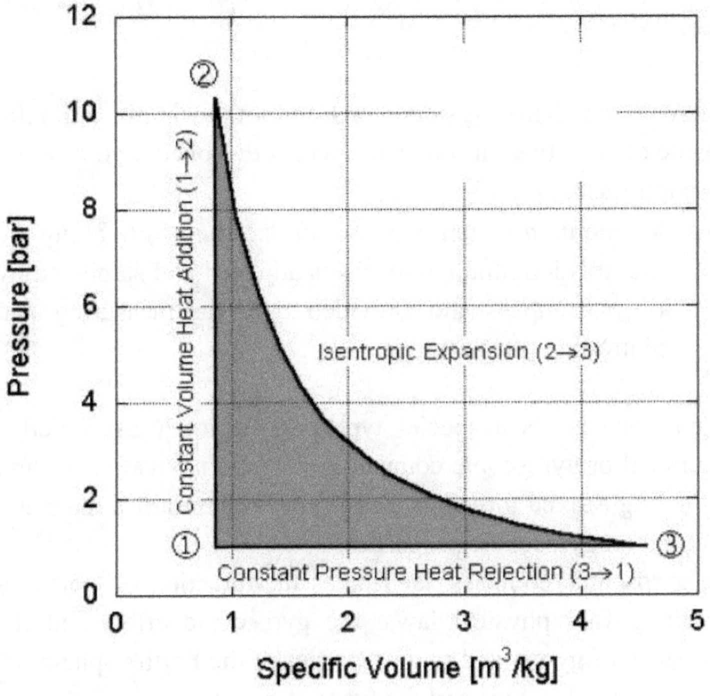

Pressure [bar]
Specific Volume [m^3/kg]
Constant Volume Heat Addition (1→2)
Isentropic Expansion (2→3)
Constant Pressure Heat Rejection (3→1)
①
②
③
0
2
4
6
8
10
12
1
3
5

System of guide

The V-1's guidance system consisted of a simple autopilot capable of adjusting altitude and speed, developed by the Berlin company Askania.

- A pendulum system that swung back and forth along the aircraft's longitudinal axis was adjusted and stabilized by a gyrocompass and provided data for measuring and controlling pitch attitude.

A gyrocompass is a special type of compass (also called a directional or gyroscopic compass), that is, a navigation system for finding a fixed direction, based not on the Earth's magnetic field, but on gyroscopic properties.
The gyroscopic compass determines the direction of North by exploiting four physical laws: the gyroscopic effect and the precession of gyros; and two properties of the Earth's sphere, its rotation around its axis and the force of gravity.
To the operating principle of the gyroscope that maintains a fixed orientation with respect to a fixed point in space, the force of gravity is added, applied with a weight on the gimbals that keep the gyroscope suspended, which, together with the other applied forces, create a precise geographic pointing.
Unlike the magnetic compass, the gyroscopic compass points towards the geographic north and is not affected by the presence of the Earth's magnetic field. Therefore, it is not subject to deviation errors (disturbances produced by disturbing magnetic fields) or those due to magnetic declination.
As a disadvantage, it requires the presence of a motor to spin and keep a rotor rotating.
Unlike the magnetic compass, it is affected by an effect called apparent precession, due to the Earth's rotation, and therefore

must be periodically realigned using a magnetic compass.

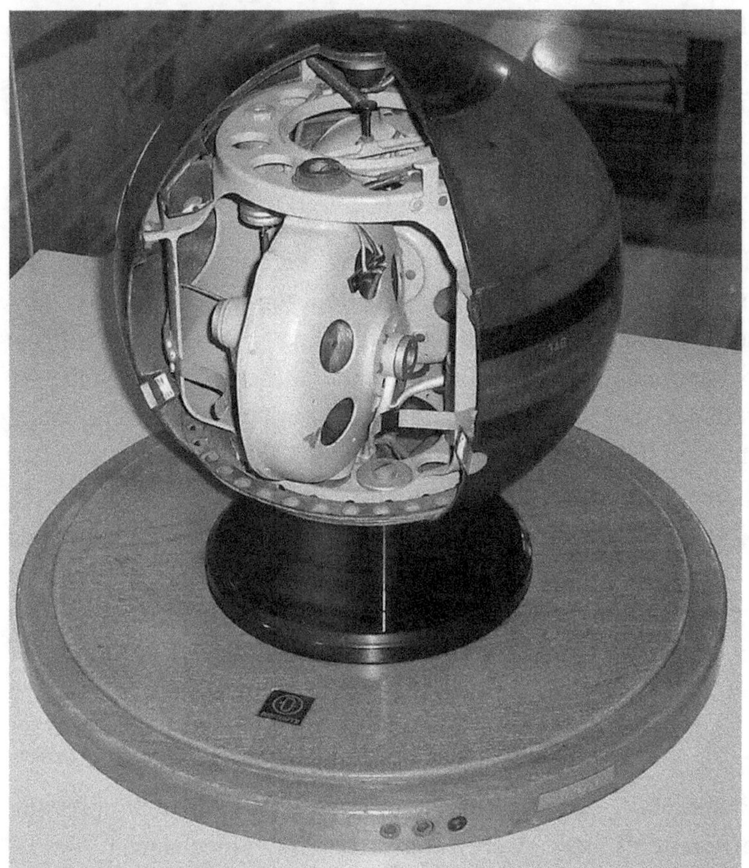

Section of the Anschütz-Kaempfe gyrocompass.

The energy needed to power both the gyroscope device both the flight control actuators were provided by two large spherical tanks loaded with compressed air before launch to 150 atmospheres (15,000 kPa) That they had also the task of pressurizing the fuel tank.

- The gyrocompass was initialized on the ground before launch and was the dedicated component providing feedback to the attitude control system.

To control yaw beyond pitch and roll, the gyro was tilted out of the horizontal plane defined by the longitudinal and roll axes, so as to react to changes in attitude on the three degrees of freedom.

- The gyroscope was kept aligned by a magnetic compass and bow and stern pendulums.

This interaction meant that changing direction required only the use of the rudder without the aid of ailerons.
In a V-1 that landed without exploding in March 1945 in the Netherlands, between Tilburg and Goirle, approximately six rolls of the Nazi propaganda magazine "Signal" were found inserted into the tubular steel spar of the left wing, used to statically balance the device before launch.

- Furthermore, it is known that many V-1s were equipped with a small radio transmitter (consisting of a triode marked 'S3', but equivalent) before launch. in a that moment at valve Of power type RL2.4T1), to check the direction Of flight Between The point of launch And the coordinate of the target respect to a r a d i o bow .

Pneumatic signals from the gyroscopes created pressure differentials that were converted into mechanical forces, opening valves for high-pressure compressed air that moved pistons in actuators for the rudder and elevators.
Roll control was by the rudder, as there were no ailerons on the wings, while altitude was controlled by an aneroid preset in millibars of atmospheric pressure.
The maximum altitude was about 3,500 metres (10,000 ft), but most bombs flew only a few thousand feet.
An odometer driven by a vane-type airspeed indicator on the nose of the aircraft determined when the target had been reached, with accuracy sufficient for bombing.

Before launch, a counter was set to a value that would reach zero upon arrival at the destination under the estimated wind conditions.

- After take-off, the air flow drove the propeller, and for every 30 rotations of the propeller the device advanced by one unit and proceeded to arm the warhead after about 60 km.

There part front with the palette anemometer, the lever Of unlock and the 4 selectors for adjustments before departure.

When the counter reached zero, two explosive bolts were detonated: the two elevator deflectors were operated, the connection between the elevator and the servo was blocked and a guillotine device cut the flexible hoses for the control of the rudder servo, leaving it free.

- These operations were intended to put the V-1 into a dive.

The dive was originally intended to be conducted with the engine at full power but in practice this maneuver resulted in the fuel flow being cut off and the engine stalling.

- The sudden silence after the classic buzz warned those present of the impending impact.

The fuel problem was later solved and the last operational examples reached their target at maximum speed.
Thanks to the counter, which determined the flight distance, the V-1 It could be launched with the ramp pointed approximately in the desired direction and the autopilot would be able to control the flight.

- The Argus pulsejet engine could not produce the thrust necessary for take-off, so the V-1 was launched using a 48-meter ramp with a 6° incline, equipped with a steam catapult system designed by the Walter company.

The ramp contained a slot fitted with a piston handle, with the flying bomb positioned on a simple trolley connected to the piston.
The piston was held in place with a pin Of safety.
The cart era constituted from a reaction chamber with tanks of 92% hydrogen peroxide (HO) and an additive consisting of

potassium permanganate (KMnO4) granules, in aqueous solution, as a catalyst, all connected to a chamber at the base of the ramp whose other end was connected to the piston.

The V-1 launch pad.

- When hydrogen peroxide was pumped into potassium permanganate, it converted into large amounts of hot steam. which built up in pressure against the piston.

When the pressure reached a certain level, 120 atmospheres, the plug the piston safety device broke and the trolley was rapidly moved up the ramp.
For the launch, only 60 liters of hydrogen peroxide and 5 liters of potassium permanganate were needed.

- The V-1 then left the launch pad at a speed of approximately 400 km/h.

On June 18, 1943, Hermann Göring decided to launch the V-1, using the Walter catapult, both from large launch bunkers, called Wasserwerk, and from lighter installations, called

Stellungsystem.

- The Wasserwerk bunker measured 215 metres (705 ft) long, 36 metres (118 ft) wide and 10 metres (33 ft) high.

Initially four were to be built: Wasserwerk Desvres, Wasserwerk St. Pol, Wasserwerk Valognes and Wasserwerk Cherbourg.

Regarding the Stellungsystem:

- Stellungsystem-I was to be operated by Flak Regiment 155(W), with 4 launch battalions, each with 4 launchers, and located in the Pas-de-Calais region.
- Stellungsystem-II, with 32 sites, was to serve as a reserve unit.
- Stellungsystem-III, operated by Flak Regiment 255(W), was to be organised in the spring of 1944 and located between Rouen and Caen.

The Stellungsystem-I and II had nine batteries equipped by February 1944.

The Stellungsystem positions included catapult walls pointed towards London, several J-shaped stowage buildings, referred to as "ski" buildings , as in aerial reconnaissance photographs the buildings looked like a ski from the side, and a compass correction building which was constructed without ferrous metal.

By the spring of 1944, Oberst Schmalschläger had developed a more simplified launch site, called Einsatz Stellungen, which was less visible, with 80 launch sites and 16 support sites located from Calais to Normandy.

Each site took just two weeks to build, using 40 men, while the Walter catapult took just 7-8 days to erect, when it was time to make it operational.

Explosives

Amatol

Amatol is an explosive mixture, consisting of ammonium nitrate and TNT.
It is made by melting TNT at about 100°C and then adding preheated powdered ammonium nitrate.
The mixture is then left to cool and a product of a more or less intense yellow colour is obtained depending on the percentage of TNT (which is yellow).
Usually its name is followed by two numbers, which indicate the proportions: for example, amatol 60/40 indicates 60% ammonium nitrate and 40% TNT.
Proportions usually range from 80/20 (80% ammonium nitrate and 20% TNT) to 50/50.
The main Amatol are 40/60 and 80/20.
Examples of other ratios that have been used are 45/55, 50/50, 83/17, and 90/10.
The mixed product has a slightly lower explosive power than pure TNT, with TNT equivalent to 0.8.
Amatol was one of the first widely used military explosives because it is insensitive to shock, heat, and cold: furthermore, amatol is relatively easy to handle.

Trialen

Trialen was the German equivalent of the British explosive Torpex, although its production was hampered by a shortage of the aluminium powder that was added to increase its explosive power.

It comprised a mixture of TNT, hexogen and aluminium powder in varying proportions for each of three versions, known respectively as trialen (or filler) 105, 106 and 107.

The proportions for each version were:

- Trialen 105: trotyl 70%, hexogen 15%, aluminium powder 15%.
- Trialen 106: trotyl 50%, hexogen 25%, aluminium powder 25%.
- Trialen 107: trotyl 50%, hexogen 20%, aluminium powder 30%.
- Trialen 105/109: a blend of 27% trialen 105 and 73% PMF 109.

PMF 109 was a mixture of 71% cyclonite, 25% aluminum powder, and 4% montan wax.

Although highly bristling and thermobaric, this mixture was infusible and rather sensitive to impact, therefore, unsuitable for filling large-caliber ammunition.

These drawbacks were overcome by the so-called Stuckfüllung, or "biscuit filling" method: the powdery mixture of PMF 109 was compressed into small, cylindrical, tablet-like pellets and these were poured into the body of the ammunition, the space between them being filled with molten trialen 105.

This method allowed German munitions factories to produce large, nearly homogeneous fillings containing a high percentage of cyclonite and, hence, high energy output by a simple variant of the smelting process, while at the same time conserving the fuel needed to do so.

Operational use

The first complete V-1 airframe was delivered on 30 August 1942. After That it was available The first motor, In September, the first test flight was carried out on 28 October 1942 near Peenemünde.

- The V-1 flew hooked under a Focke-Wulf Fw 200.

For the first flight test with a working engine, however, we had to wait until December 10, when an example was dropped from an He-111 bomber, which was carrying it attached to its lower part.
A myth relates that the stabilization and guidance problems were solved thanks to a daring test flight carried out by the famous aviator Hanna Reitsch, who personally piloted a V-1 specially modified for flying. humans.

- Conventional launch sites could theoretically launch about fifteen V-1s a day. This, however, was a rate that was difficult to maintain, at least on homogeneous base. However, the maximum reached was eighteen.

Overall, only 15% of the bombs hit their target, with the majority being lost due to Allied countermeasures, mechanical problems or guidance errors.
The operational ceiling was initially planned to be around 2,750 metres; however, due to repeated problems with the barometric pressure regulator of the fuel, the Germans were forced to lower this ceiling in May 1944, effectively putting the V-1 within range of the 40 mm Bofors guns, widely used by Allied anti-aircraft units.
The versions Of trial from the V-1 were air dropped.
In operational conditions, most of the ordnance was launched

from fixed land installations (Calais and the Dutch coast), although between July 1944 and January 1945, there Luftwaffe no he threw approximately 1,176 examples of modified Heinkel He 111 bombers, belonging to Kampfgeschwader 3 which operated over the North Sea.
Besides the obvious reason to continue the bombing campaign even after the loss of the land installations on the French coast, the airdrop provided the Luftwaffe with the opportunity to circumvent the increasingly effective countermeasures put in place by the Allies to counter this type of weapon, as well as to increase their range.

To minimize the risks associated with these operations (especially that of being detected by radar), the crews Germans they developed a tactics call "lo-hi-lo": the He-111s were supposed to, after leaving their air bases and passing the coast, descend to a very low flight altitude. After reaching the launch point, the crews were supposed to regain altitude, drop the device, and quickly descend to the previous altitude, in order to return.

- Research after the war they demonstrated That there percentage Of failures era by 40%, and the He-111s used for this purpose were extremely vulnerable to night fighters: this was due to the fact that the brightness produced by the departure of the V1 illuminated the area around the carrier aircraft for some seconds.

Another project involved a ventral fuel tank adaptation to be used on the Messerschmitt Me 262 fighters.

In this case the As 014 engine, internal systems and warhead were removed leaving only the wing panels and the airframe which now contained only a large fuel tank.

A small cylindrical module, similar in shape to a dart without fins, was positioned atop the vertical stabilizer at the rear of the tank and served as the center of gravity balance and attachment point for a variety of equipment: a rigid tow bar and, at the front end, a pitch pivot provided the connection between the two aircraft.

- The use of this unusual configuration involved the adoption of a wheeled trolley, connected under the V1-tank to facilitate take-off and which detached once in flight.

Once the fuel was exhausted, it was separated from the tow bar by a series of explosive bolts.

In 1944 a series of flight tests were conducted, but a serious problem with the fuel tank trim was found, which tended to "porpoising", an instability that was also transferred to the fighter, making the combination too unreliable to be used. A similar combination was also attempted with the Arado Ar 234, but the same problem recurred and development was abandoned in this case too.

On some of these V1-tanks, the adoption of a conspicuous fixed faired landing gear was experimented with but, in addition to being useless, it contributed to increasing aerodynamic resistance as well as worsening the overall stability of the assembly.

Only one variant of the original Fi 103 design reached operational use.

From 1944, due to the progressive loss of launch sites on French territory and the general reduction of the territory under German control, the V-1 soon lost its ability to reach targets in England.

- Although the possibility of air launching had been developed, a development was planned that would increase the range of the device, identified as F1.

The capacity of the weapon's fuel tank was therefore increased, with a corresponding reduction in the mass of the warhead. In addition, the front part of the fuselage, which in the V-1 was metal, was replaced with a wooden nose cone, a solution that offered a significant saving in weight. With these modifications, the V-1 was able to reach London and nearby urban centers from emplacements in the Netherlands.

High priority was given to building enough F-1s to support a major bombing campaign to coincide with the start of the Ardennes Offensive, but a number of factors (the bombing of the factories that produced the missiles, the shortage of available steel, the lack of a rail network for their transport, the chaotic tactical situation that Germany was facing at that time of the conflict) delayed the delivery of this V-1 until it became available only between February and March 1945.

Before the V-1-based attack campaign was finally concluded at the end of March, several hundred F-1s had reached Britain launched from Dutch sites.

During there war, no they came products over 30,000 examples; each of these required 350 hours of work (including

120 for the autopilot), at a cost that was 4% of that of a V-2, with a comparable war load (830 kg charge of high-explosive Amatol, or TNT). and ammonium nitrate, but sometimes a cheaper type of explosive, Danarit, was used).

- The first flying bomb fell on Swanscombe, near Gravesend, located on the Thames, east of London, on 13 June 1944 at 4.18am; this first bomb fell in a field, leaving a crater about 5 metres (16 ft) in diameter and almost 1 metre (3 ft) deep.

Although it caused no casualties, it seriously damaged a house. That same Night they were throw only a dozen V-1s, contrary to what the German General Staff had predicted:

- Two hours before of dawn, launch Of 300 V- 1.
- At noon, launch of 100 V-1s and in the afternoon 2-3 launches every hour.
- There evening, a fed launch Of V-1 as curfew.
- In the first 10 days, 370 V-1 they hit London.

Well Soon there answer came organized And the hunting They went to intercept flying bombs over the English Channel, as well as responding with anti-aircraft fire and installing barrage balloons on the outskirts of London.

These measures began to bear fruit, as in one day, out of 97 V-1s launched by the Germans, only 4 hit London. The English were also asked not to specify the nature of the death in the newspaper obituaries, to avoid giving directions to the Germans who did not have precise information about the crash site of the flying bombs.

Furthermore, The against espionage began to transmit false information about the fall of the V-1s, communicating with accuracy the number of bombs that fell too far from the initial target, while for those that reached the target, false information was communicated corresponding to places far from the city centre.

A Spitfire (right) attempts an interception manoeuvre and closes in on a V-1 to tip it over with its wing, in a famous photograph taken over Britain.

- Overall, England it was reached from approximately 10,000 such devices: the capital London, in particular, was hit 3,564 times, killing 6,184 people and injuring a further 17,981.
- The highest density of V-1s fell near Croydon, located south-east of the city.
- Another 1,600 were pulled by He-111H-22s.
- Of the missiles, 1,847 were shot down by fighters such as P-51s, Spitfires and others, 10-12 by naval guns, 232 by balloon braking cables, 1,878 from anti-aircraft guns.
- 31,600 homes were destroyed and over a million were damaged.

The victims British caused come on German bombers had numbered around 51,509, but by now the Germans could no longer afford bombing campaigns with conventional aircraft.
But the British had not only suffered casualties and damage to civilians: it seems that the factories hit, considering only those with strategic interests, were 50 in the capital, and 919 in other

regions, which required 6.5 million man-hours and 21,000 people, with a drop in production of 10% of the industry English.

- If the data officers they speak of 275,000 people evicted from London, in reality the data known since 1994 say 1,450,000, so the workforce was greatly reduced.

The loss to the Air Ministry was specified at £47.6 million, plus 450 aircraft and 2,900 men lost in counter-bombing actions (perhaps including ground attack actions on the ramps).

- A large-scale bombing operation on Peenemunde was launched by the RAF on the night of 17/18 August 1943 (Operation Hydra) using 597 bombers (324 Lancasters, 219 Halifaxes and 54 Stirlings), of which 94 were Pathfinders. (the unit specials in charge Of report with bombs bright The goals) That they would have due hit, in sequence, the scientists' residences, two large factories, the design workshops and the administrative offices.

Pilot John Searby was put in charge of all this.
This raid killed some 700 people, including Walter Thiel, head of engine development.
This raid prompted the V-1 rocket production to move underground. Despite the raids, many Peenemünde installations remained intact at the end of World War II, as most of the bombs were dropped on the housing areas and camps of foreign workers.
There is much controversy over how the Allies discovered the existence of Peenemünde.

- The official British version stated that all the information was gathered through aerial reconnaissance.

However, testimonies and documents claim that the intelligence of the Polish underground army (Armia Krajowa or AK) and information from other sources (including a Danish pilot That he photographed something That looked like to a rocket V) revealed Peenemünde.

British intelligence denied for years that it had received any information about Peenemünde from Poland.

However, copies of the reports surfaced in Poland after the war; RV Jones contradicted himself: first he denied the fact, later in his book "The Wizard War" wrote that many bombs fell on the workers' fields foreigners That they gave information to the allies; he did not say that these Polish workers belonged to the AK.

In recent years Polish politicians and historians have called for Of access the archives British (so long as The UK holds many, if not all, of the AK reports).

Currently the British authorities have responded that all AK reports were destroyed.

- On July 18, 1944 and August 4, it was the turn of 413 Boeing B-17 " Flying Fortresses."

The research center suffered heavy damage from the 1,600 tons of bombs unhooked, However, someone constructions important were saved, as well as the related archives, allowing operations to continue, after having taken steps to camouflage the factories. However, aware that these factories were no longer safe from the bombings, Hitler ordered the installation of the V1 production workshops under the mountains, installing them near Nordhausen, in the Mittelwerk, under the Harz mountain (code name Dora) and of use concentration camp manpower, under the direction of German technicians, in order to prevent information leaks.

The underground was a old mine Of carbonates of calcium (gypsum), exploited since the 1920s, and made up of two parallel tunnels 1,800 metres long and 46 transverse tunnels 150 metres long (this was the distance between the two tunnels main).

- The project consisted of leave the two tunnels as service roads, with railways for the port and the collection of materials, and to build workshops in the 46 tunnels.

They came facts arrive (September 1943) from Buchenwald, 17,000 deportees who immediately set to work (cleaning and concreting the tunnels).
The speed of the decisions makes the problem of housing the deportees pass into the background, who, in six months, see the sun twice during the disinfestations: they are infested with lice; they have no water to drink, they breathe ammonia fumes that burn their lungs, so much so that in six months as many as 6,500 deportees die.
Finally, in February 1944, Albert Speer gets The permit Of visit the concentration camp.
Yes says stay shocked from the situation; ago understand to the SS that it is counterproductive to teach the trade if after a few months it was necessary to start all over again; he ordered that the external camp be built immediately; he sent wagons of material, other deportees from Buchenwald were brought in and in a month 56 barracks were built scattered around the camp: everything was fenced off with barbed wire with high-voltage electricity.

Finally the deportees, after 12 hours of work, can leave the tunnels, wash themselves and sleep in the bunks.

- There mortality decreases, there cadence of exit of the missiles becomes regular (500/550 to the month), 2,000 of which were dropped on London between June and July 1944 and 1,000 on Antwerp.

The Allied air force, of course, cannot bomb the tunnels and so

it destroys bridges, railways, roads; it razes the city of Nordhausen, where there are missile component factories; it bombs a factory in Buchenwald, causing 364 deaths in the camp.
The rate of missile releases decreases until it stops completely; then the SS begins to wall up the entrances to the tunnels, because none of the deportees who built the missiles must survive.
But the population of Nordhausen, terrified by the constant bombing, forced the entrances to the camp and took refuge in the tunnels, thwarting the SS' plan.
Then the so-called marches of the death, because none of the deportees must survive.
Finally, on April 14, 1945, the Americans arrive.
The commander is accompanied by some survivors into the tunnels: he discovers a hundred missiles and tons of blueprints; he warns the command. The order is to restore a line railway, Yes from there hunting to the 500 technicians, including von Braun and the General, and all of this, at the end of June, comes embarked in Antwerp and left for the United States.

- Out with the Americans, the Russians are coming. They also inspect the tunnels: they find some missiles forgotten by the Americans; but they come into possession of an unexpected gift left involuntarily by those who preceded them: tons of construction plans, a godsend for the Russian designers.

After which the entrances are mined and destroyed and no one is allowed in. more to know what had happened: and the silence lasts for 53 years, because neither one nor the other had any interest in making it known that their space exploits were the result of everything they had stolen from the Dora tunnels, despite the protests of the survivors who had urged their governments to shed light on that concentration camp.

Finally, in 1998, in number 26 from the famous magazine German “Stern”, dozens of colour photographs of the Dora camp appear, with the deportees working in the tunnels.
What had happened?
The Nazis had photographers everywhere; even in Dora's galleries there was a photographer: he had stolen dozens of slides, hidden in a package in his suitcase.
After there war, Perhaps For some poorly concealed fear, if he had returned home and hidden the briefcase in the garage.
In 1998, now 91 years old, he was admitted to a retirement home: his son went to clear out his father's house and found the slides in his suitcase in the garage.

- At the end of the war Von Braun was working on the project of a missile, the V-3, capable of hitting New York. He did not have time to realize it, the Third Reich collapsed first.

The young engineer knew he ran the risk of being considered a war criminal and ending up in Nuremberg, even though he had worked to the dependencies of the army And Not from the SS. But he also knew that the Americans would forgive him anything as long as he joined their side.
Thus in Reutte, a small village in Tyrol, he surrendered to US troops with a hundred collaborators and the Peenemunde facilities, which were promptly taken from the Soviets.
He was welcomed with full honors and by 1950 he was already an American citizen. From September 1944, however, the threat of the V -1 to England was temporarily interrupted, due to the loss (capture or destruction) of the French coastal installations from which the launches were carried out.

- For this reason, the V-1 was subsequently used mainly to attack strategic targets in Belgium (especially the port of Antwerp): between October 1944 and March 1945, The Village, overall, it was hit from 2,448 devices.

- V-1s destroyed by fighters, anti-aircraft guns and there were 4,261 barrage balloons.

The last V-1 fell in England on 29 March 1945, at Datchworth in Hertfordshire: it was the last enemy action on English soil of the Second World War.
The English Defence against the weapons German to long ray it was called Operation Crossbow.
Anti-aircraft guns were redeployed in several moves: first in mid-June 1944 from positions on the North Downs to the south coast of England, then along a cordon closing off the Thames to attacks from the east.

- In September 1944, a new line of defence was laid out on the East Anglian coast, and finally in December a new defensive configuration was adopted along the coast between Lincolnshire and Yorkshire.

The deployments were conditioned by the changes to the V-1 approach lines as the launch sites had been reached by the Allied advance. On the first night of bombing, the anti-aircraft troops near Croydon rejoiced: unexpectedly, an unprecedented number of German bombers had been shot down, most of the targets having been set ablaze or having been hit in the engine , crashing.
However, there was great disappointment when another truth became apparent. Anti-aircraft gunners soon discovered that these small, fast-moving targets were, in fact, extremely difficult from hit. The altitude Of cruise of the V-1, between 600 and 900 meters, was slightly greater than the effective range of light anti-aircraft guns and just below the height optimal of engagement of the heavy antiaircraft.
Other countermeasures included barrage balloons and the use of interceptor fighters.

- Some RAF pilots, such as Jean Maridor, used an original

system to destroy the V-1s without using the weapons of their fighters; in fact, approaching the V-1, they positioned their wing under the wing of the bomb and progressively, acting with the ailerons, destabilized it by modifying its trajectory to make it fall into the sea or in any case far from inhabited centers.

This method was developed by Pilot Officer Johnny Faulkner, operating in the 91st Squadron, the same as Jean Maridor.

- Another method was to switch to speed maximum very close at the V-1 That could be so unbalanced by the propeller turbulence.

The aircraft used were:

- Supermarine Spitfire XIVs of 91 Squadron which destroyed 189 V-1s.
- Hawker Typhoons of 137 Squadron which shot down 30 flying bombs.
- The Hawker Tempests of the 602nd Squadron commanded, at the end of the war, by the flying ace Pierre Clostermann which destroyed 481 V-1s.

Before the end of the war, the Americans began modifying and copying the V-1 from salvaged parts supplied to them by the British and built more than 1,000 US versions called the JB-2, and popularly known as the Thunderbug, which were to be used against both the Germans and the Japanese.
Ford Motor Company built the pulsejet engines, while Republic Aviation built the airframes and parts of the Willys-Overland airframe.

- None of these missiles entered combat, although they provided missile experience to both the Army Air Forces and the Navy.

The Air Forces tested several ground and air launches of the JB-2, beginning in October 1944 at Eglin Air Field (later AFB), Florida.
The air drops were made, one under each wing, from Boeing B-17G Flying Fortresses, with the intention of also using them with the B-29 Superfortress. The Navy version, designated Loon and also KUW-1, was tested at Point Mugu, California, later launched from submarines in the Pacific.

- After the war, thanks to the V-1, the pulsejet was also in vogue for several years as a low-cost powerplant for a variety of subsonic missiles and target drones in the United States and other countries.

For example, the French Arsenal ARS 5501 was a radio-controlled surface-to-air or air-to-air drone developed in 1949 and closely resembled the original V-1.
When air-launched, the ARS 5501 was mounted and launched from a LeO 45 aircraft. Post-war American pulsejet-powered aircraft included the XKD5G-1 and Katydid drones and the Gorgon 2C missiles: these aircraft, however, soon became obsolete as they were unable to operate at high altitudes and at higher speeds.

Versions

There V-1 came built in versions different:

- **I.E. 103 A1**

Version standard.

- **FI 103 A2**

Modified version of the A1 with a pulse jet that conferred a speed of about 800 km/h.

- **FI 103 B1**

This was an upgraded turbojet-powered variant, intended to use the low-cost Porsche 109.005 turbojet engine with a thrust of around 500 kgf (1,100 lbf).
It featured a wooden nose cone, fuel tanks increased from 602 to 689 litres and an increase in wingspan to 5.74 metres.

- Design of the Porsche 005 began in late 1944 with the goal of providing a more fuel-efficient engine for the V-1 while allowing for greater ranges.

The use of the Porsche 005 turbojet was designed to increase the V-1's range from 240 km (149 mi) to 700 km (435 mi) and allow launch without a launch pad.
During the final months of World War II, the Porsche 005 project was led by Dr. Max Adolf Mueller, who had worked on jet engine designs for both Junkers and Heinkel. Dr. Mueller was taken prisoner at the end of the war and later prepared a drawing of the Porsche 005 for American investigators.

- **FI 103 B2**

With explosive Trialen 105 or 106 “albuminized” to increase potency.

- **FI 103 A1 RE1**

This version was developed between late 1944 and early 1945 for launching over Holland.
The range was increased to 300 km with the addition of a petrol tank. more big to the detriment of the charge explosive which had been reduced.

- **FI 103 D-1**

Intent to use chemical aggressive agents, which however was not realized.

- **Reichenberg RE I and II**

A single-seater without an engine, it was towed like a glider.

- **Reichenberg RE III**

Two-seater with pulse jet, intended for training.

- **Reichenberg RE IV**

Single-seater with pulse jet.
This was the version that was to become operational.
More than 175 units were built, but they were never put into service.
Towards the end of the conflict a good number of number of V-

1s equipped with a cockpit, modified to allow control by volunteer pilots, known as Reichenbergs.
None of these were used in combat missions.

- These aircraft retained the general characteristics of the device from which they were derived but, unlike the V-1s, take-off did not occur via a launch pad but using mother aircraft, with release in flight.

After an initial phase of development and flight testing, a problem arose that the technical department could not explain: several test pilots called to test the aircraft's characteristics in flight were killed because they were unable to complete the landing maneuver.

- In an attempt to resolve the anomaly, Hanna Reitsch was contacted and started a series of test flights at end to find the cause.

There Reitsch performed a series of simulated high-altitude landings, repeating the operations Suggested For the landing using the airspace to gain time to recall the aircraft, discovering that the Fi 103R had an extremely high stall speed and that the previous pilots, who did not They had experience in high-speed flight, they approached this phase at too low a speed.

- His recommendation was, therefore, to maintain a much higher landing speed, a maneuver later introduced into the formation. of the self-stopping, the pilots volunteers destined at 5.Staffel of the Combat unit 200, known Also like Leonidas Squadron.

The planning of the missions, which were never put into practice, included the use of the bomber to jet Plowed Ar 234 either as a tow aircraft, connected to the Reichenberg with a rope, or in an inverted mistel configuration with the aircraft resting on its back.

Model of an Arado Ar 234 carrying a V-1 at the Technikmuseum Speyer.

In this last configuration, a hydraulically controlled device operated by the pilot, it had the task of lifting the Fi 103R about eight metres from its seat, an operation necessary to avoid damaging the upper part of the mother aircraft when its own Argus As 014 pulse jet was turned on and to ensure an airflow free from the turbulence caused by the Ar 234's jet engines.

- A less ambitious project involved an adaptation to a ventral tank Of fuel from to match to the hunting Messerschmitt Me 262.

In this case the As 014 engine, internal systems and warhead were removed leaving only the wing panels and the airframe which now contained only a large fuel tank.

A small cylindrical module, similar in shape to a dart without fins, was positioned atop the vertical stabilizer at the rear of the tank and served as the center of gravity balance and attachment point for a variety of equipment.

The two aircraft were connected by a rigid tow bar and, at the front end, a pitch pivot. The use of this unusual configuration involved the use of a wheeled trolley, attached under the V1-tank to facilitate take-off and which detached once in flight. Once the fuel was exhausted, it was separated from the tow bar by a series of explosive bolts.

- In 1944 a series of flight tests were conducted, but a serious trim problem was encountered. tank that tended to "porpoising", an instability that also transferred to the fighter, making the combination too unreliable to be used.

A similar combination was also attempted with the Arado Ar 234 but the same problem arose and development of this aircraft was abandoned as well.
On some of these V1-tank came experienced the adoption Of a showy cart fixed faired but, in addition to be useless, contributed to increase aerodynamic resistance as well as worsen the overall stability of the assembly.

- Only one variant of the original Fi 103 design reached operational use.

From 1944, due to the progressive loss of launch sites on French territory and the general reduction of the territory under German control, the V-1 soon lost its ability to reach targets in England.

- Although the possibility of air-dropping had been developed, a development was planned that would increase the range of the device, identified as F-1.

The capacity of the weapon's fuel tank was increased, with a corresponding reduction in the mass of the warhead. In addition, the front part of the fuselage, which in the V-1 was metal, was replaced with a wooden nose cone, a solution that offered a significant saving in weight.

- With these modifications the V-1 was able to reach London and nearby urban centers from positions in the Netherlands.

Top priority was given to building enough F-1s to ensure a major bombing campaign to coincide with the start of the Ardennes Offensive, but several factors (the bombing of the factories that produced the missiles, the shortage of available steel, the lack of a network for their rail transport, the chaotic tactical situation that Germany was facing at that time of the conflict) delayed the delivery of this V-1 making it available only between February and March 1945.

- Before the V-1 attack campaign was finally concluded at the end of March, several hundred F-1s reached Britain from Dutch sites.

One example is located at the Imperial War Museum in London. Another example is located at the Science Museum in London. In Paris, it can be admired at the Musée de l'Armée.

- There V-1 it was Also copied from others, to example by the US Navy who intended to make it a bombing system against the Japanese coasts, the Willys - Overland JB-2/KGW/KUW/LTV-A-1/LTV-N-2 Loon, which was developed from July 1944, when the wreckage of a V -1 was brought to the United States.

The new bomb took many months to be considered reliable but the USAAF developed a radio guidance system with a radar “beacon” to help locate the missile and final radio command for the dive: it was estimated that this could improve accuracy, and indeed at 160 km 400 metres were achieved, at least an order of magnitude greater.

They came facts Also throws from a B-17 And Yes they put

orders for 75,000 missiles, but the invasion of Japan did not take place.
The “Thunderbug”, called Like this from the USAAF, came completed in 1,391 units.
In December 1944, eight out of ten launches failed; but in June, 128 out of 164 were successful, while it was estimated that between 1,000 and 5,000 would be produced per month.
This was certainly not a result of a “failure” weapon as Allied propaganda had portrayed it. The US Navy , instead, wanted to launch them from escort carriers, but later tested them from two submarines, contributing to the development of the Regulus missile.
The Loon's features were:

- Weight: 2,270 kg
- 907 kg of head
- 360kgs pulse jet
- Speed of 685 km/h.

Technical Features

Dimensions and weights

- Weight: 2,150 kg
- Length: 8.32 meters
- Height: 1.42 meters

Performance

- Vectors: Heinkel He 111
- Range: 250 km
- Tangency: 2,750 meters (theoretical)
- Speed maximum: 640 km/h
- Motor: a Argus pulse jet As 014
- Fuel: gas 80 octane
- Fuel tank: 640 litres
- Cost: $ 500
- Header: 850 kg of explosives Amatol-39 (or Danarit) with three fuses:

  - ❖ An electric fuse was triggered by impact with the nose or belly.

  - ❖ Another fuse was a slow-acting mechanical fuse, which allowed deeper penetration into the ground, regardless of altitude.

  - ❖ The third fuse was a delayed-action fuse, set to explode two hours after launch.

The purpose of the third fuse was to avoid the risk of this secret weapon being examined by the British.
Its delay was intended to destroy the weapon if a soft landing had not activated the impact fuzes. These fuze systems were very reliable and almost no defective V-1s were recovered.

Fieseler Fi 103R

The Fieseler Fi 103R, initially known as the Reichenberg, was a single-seat, medium-wing military aircraft, which can be defined as a manned flying bomb, produced by the German company Gerhard-Fieseler-Werke GmbH in the 1940s.

- Era a piloted version of the Wunderwaffe V-1.

Developed as part of the Luftwaffe's volunteer special unit 5.Staffel of Kampfgeschwader 200, also known as the Leonidas Squadron, it was part of a kamikaze mission program planned in the last phase of the Second World War but never entered the operational phase.
Towards the end of the Second World War, the war situation adverse to Germany was becoming increasingly worrying and it became necessary for the military authorities to urge the war industry to find a solution to reverse the fortunes of the conflict.

- In this context, the possibility of establishing special units made up of volunteer pilots capable of contributing to operational suicide missions was also evaluated.

For this purpose, on direct suggestion Of Adolf Hitler, came a new squadron was created within the Kampfgeschwader 200, The 5.Staffel better known such as Leonidas Squadron, where pilots were required to sign a document in which they stated:

- *"I hereby voluntarily request to be enrolled in the suicide group as part of a manned bomb glider. I fully understand that operational employment in this capacity will result in my death."*

Initially, both the Messerschmitt Me 328 and the Fieseler Fi 103 (better known as the V-1 flying bomb), suitably modified, were considered suitable equipment, but after a comparative evaluation, the former combined with a 900 kg bomb was preferred.

Fieseler Fi 103R.

The Messerschmitt Me 328 was a jet fighter project designed in Germany by Messerschmitt towards the end of World War II.

- The Me 328 was originally designed to be dropped from a bomber to protect it from enemy interceptors, with the possibility of subsequent recovery.

Several companies collaborated in its production: the DFS (Deutsche Forschungsanstalt für Segelflug) built several engineless prototypes, which performed numerous towed flights, and the pre-series aircraft was assembled at Jacobs-Schweyer.

After several modifications to the design, in the autumn of 1943 the prototype began its trials as a glider, launched by a Dornier Do 17 which carried it on its back to the required altitude.

- Power tests were carried out with two 300 kgp Argus As 014 reactors placed in the rear part of the fuselage, but they presented serious problems.

The conversion, therefore, it proved difficult to point that Heinrich Himmler thought it was more appropriate to cancel the project. However, Hitler, convinced of the usefulness of the department, contacted Otto Skorzeny to relaunch its activity, thanks to the experience acquired in studies regarding the possibility of using manned torpedoes against Allied naval units. Feasibility studies were started on the V-1 to which It was given the code name "Projekt Reichenberg" (after Reichenberg, the capital of the historical Czechoslovakian region Sudetenland, now known as Liberec).

- The development of the "Reichenberg-Geräte" (Reichenberg equipment), as the Fi 103R was called, involved a series of modifications to the V-1, the most visible of which was the adoption of a cockpit closed by a removable canopy, a solution that was preferred in order to give, in any case, a chance of salvation to the pilot engaged in the attack mission.

In the summer of 1944, the Deutsche Forschungsanstalt für Segelflug (DFS), the gliding research institute based in Ainring, took on the task of developing the version piloted of the V-1 succeeding to realize in Alone a few days a specimen to be used for testing and installation a production line at Dannenberg.
The V-1 was transformed into the Reichenberg by inserting a small cockpit into the cell in the position immediately forward of the pulse jet air intake, where the standard V-1 housed the compressed air tanks.

- Although around 70 examples were built for use by the KG 200 special unit, none were actually used operationally and development stopped in October 1944.

The cockpit was basic, equipped with minimal flight

instrumentation (five instruments: an arming switch, a clock, an airspeed indicator, an altimeter and a turn and vacuum indicator) and a bucket seat made of plywood, enclosed by a canopy, made in a single piece, which incorporated a front armoured panel and a side opening to allow access to the pilot.
A simple gunsight was supposed to help align the target, while the dive angles marked on the side window provided the pilot with final indications before abandoning the aircraft.
After reaching his target, the pilot would have to aim accurately and then eject, somehow avoiding the suction of the pulsejet behind him. There was no landing gear.

- The front part of the Fi 103R-IV was packed with 800 kg of explosives.

The two compressed air tanks were replaced by a single one, mounted at the rear, occupying the space that normally housed the autopilot in the V-1.

- The wings were modified by integrating edges metallic in degree Of cut the cables of the balloons of damming.

The proposal put forward was that the aircraft should be carried by a mother aircraft, a Heinkel He 111 bomber, capable of attaching one or two under the wings and releasing them in the vicinity of the target.
The pilot would have flown it to the target, releasing the canopy just before reaching it and bailing out with the parachute; however, the proximity of the engine air intake compromised the ease of the operation, to the point that the calculation of the percentage of survival of the pilots was environment at 1%.
In fact, to release the canopy, it was necessary to operate a lever on the left side of the cockpit, at the estimated approach speed of 645 km/h.

- There training of the pilots was starting on conventional

gliders, to give them the ability to manage the aircraft during gliding flight, then continuing on special gliders, modified by adopting a canopy with a reduced wingspan and capable of performing dive maneuvers reaching 300 km/h.

A exemplary Of self-stopping, a Fieseler Fi 103.

The third phase included training on the R-II, the two-seater variant of the Reichenberg. Advanced training was carried out on the RI and R-II and, although the landing maneuver on the ventral skid was difficult, the models proved to have good flight behavior. For which Yes he hypothesized That the self-stopping, the pilots volunteers destined for the Leonidas Squadron, could soon be in degree Of to carry out missions operational.

Albert Speer, in a dispatch sent to Hitler on July 28, 1944, suggested not to waste men and resources on targets on French soil and that they would be more effective against power plants on Soviet territory.

For what can be considered the first real flight we had to wait until September 1944, when a Reichenberg was dropped from an He 111 in the skies above Larz.

- The flight, however, proved to be a failure as the aircraft crashed after the pilot lost control due to the accidental activation of the canopy detachment device.

The second flight, carried out the following day, also ended in an accident.

The accidents continued one after another, a problem that the technical department did not he was able to explain himself: several test pilots called to test the characteristics of the aircraft in flight were killed because they were unable to complete the landing maneuver.

- In an attempt to resolve the anomaly, Heinz Kensche and Hanna Reitsch were contacted and began a series of test flights to find the cause.

Both were involved in some accidents from which, however, they emerged unharmed.

On November 5, 1944, during the second test flight of the R-III, a wing section broke off due to vibrations, however, Kensche managed to activate the safety parachute albeit with some difficulty. due to the small size of the passenger compartment.

Reitsch performed a series of simulated high-altitude landings, repeating the suggested landing operations using the airspace to give herself time to recall. the aircraft, discovering that the Fi 103R possessed a speed Of extremely deadlock high And that the previous pilots, who had no experience of high-speed flight, approached this phase at too low a speed.

- His recommendation was, Therefore, Of maintain a speed of a much higher landing, a maneuver later introduced in the Selbstopfer formation.

After Werner Baumbach took over command of KG 200 in October 1944, he made the decision to shelve the development of the Reichenberg in favor of the Mistel project.

Baumbach and Speer finally managed to have a meeting with

Hitler on March 15, 1945 where they argued that suicide missions were not part of German military traditions, convincing him to approve their suspension.

Later that day, Baumbach ordered the disbandment of the Reichenberg unit.

Technical Features

Specimens: approximately 175

Dimensions and weights

- Length: 8.00 meters
- Wingspan: 5,715 meters
- Fuselage diameter: 0.838 meters
- Load weight: 2,250 kg

Propulsion

- Engine: one Argus As 014 pulse jet
- Thrust: 3.4 kN (350 kg)

Performance

- Max speed:c 650 km/h (800 km/h in dive)
- Autonomy: 330 km

Versions

- **Fi 103R-I**

Single-seater training version, without engine.

- **Fi 103R-II**

Two-seater training version with the second cockpit positioned where the warhead was normally located.

- **Fi 103R-III**

Single-seat training version, equipped with only the pulse jet air intake for training launch operations.

- **Fi 103R-IV**

Standard operating version.

Bachem Ba 349

The Bachem Ba 349 Natter was an experimental rocket-powered interceptor fighter built by the German company Bachem-Werke GmbH in the 1940s and used operationally, much like surface-to-air missiles, in the final stages of World War II.
Most of the flight to the bombers was guided by radio control from the ground and the pilot then had to land with a parachute.

- Built with limited use of strategic materials, the aircraft represented one of the wunderwaffen developed for look for Of subvert the decline German in evolving of the conflict.

With the Luftwaffe's air superiority seriously tested by the Allies over the skies of the Reich in 1943, to avoid there crisis they came requests from the innovations radicals.
Surface-to-air missiles seemed to be a very promising approach to counter the Allied bomber offensive and several projects were started, but various problems with the guidance system prevented their widespread use. Equipping the missile with a pilot which could control the weapon during the critical final phase of flight seemed to be the best solution and this specification was requested by the Luftwaffe in early 1944.
A large number of simple designs were proposed, most of which featured the pilot in a prone position to reduce the frontal section.
The main candidate for the specification was initially the Heinkel P.1077 which took off from a launch pad and landed on a sled much like the Messerschmitt Me 163 Komet.
Erich Bachem's BP20 was a development from a project which he was working on in Fieseler, but considerably more radical

than the other proposals.
It was built using wooden parts glued and screwed onto an armoured cockpit, pushed from a rocket Walter HWK 109-509A-2 to liquid propellant , similar to that of the Me 163. Four Schmidding rockets were used for take-off, for a total thrust of 4,800 kgf (47 kN) for 10 seconds after being states started.

- The plane took off from a ramp Of about 25 meters, necessary to reach a speed enough to operate the aerodynamic controls to be able to control it.

The aircraft took off and was guided from the ground to the altitude of the Allied bombers by radio control, with the pilot taking control only long enough to point the nose in the right direction, release the plastic hull and pull the trigger.
The latter fired a salvo of rockets (33 R4M or 24 Hs 217), after which the aircraft flew over the bombers.

- After exhausting its fuel, the aircraft was to be used to hit the tail of a bomber, with the pilot parachuting to the ground just before impact.

Despite its apparent complexity, the design had one decisive advantage over its opponents: it eliminated the need to land a high-speed rocket plane at an air base that, as the history of the Me 163 demonstrated, was extremely vulnerable to Allied air raids.
After Bachem's design had attracted the attention of Heinrich Himmler at the SS command, he became the official winner of the specification.
The Luftwaffe, however, planned to include some minor reworks to try to salvage as much of the aircraft as possible, for example, eliminating the final impact attack.
The resulting small aircraft was to be fired from a 15-meter wooden ramp with the help of four solid-fuel rockets, at the end

of which it would reach the speed required to operate its control surfaces.

- The rockets would have shut down after 12 seconds, after which the main engine would have been brought up to full power. push.

To this point the mission would have had to bring The aircraft to a position in front of And above enemy bombers , where the pilot would have turned off the autopilot, and it would be went down for a gliding attack.

A Bachem Ba349, with open cockpit and bow rockets on display.

After firing its rocket armament it would continue to to glide to high speed until to a share of 3,000 meters, after which the plane would have "broken" due to the opening of a large parachute at the rear of the aircraft, separating it from the front part with the pilot.

Both sides would have landed with their separate parachutes, and the fuselage with the wooden wings would have been lost.

The fuselage length was 6.02 metres and consisted of three parts:

- The nose housed the rockets and the cockpit.
- The central part housed the fuel tanks and the wings which were made of wood and had a single spar, also made of wood, which ran from one end of the wing to the other across the entire fuselage. The wings had no movable control surfaces.
- Finally, the rear part housed the rocket engine and a cruciform tail equipped with movable surfaces to ensure control of the machine.

The BP-20 prototypes and the pre-production Ba-349A were equipped with a special version of the HWK 109-509A-2 single-chamber rocket engine.

- The propellants (750 kg) for this rocket engine were hydrogen peroxide ($H_2 0_2$) as the oxidizer and a hydrazine/methanol mixture as the fuel.

Hydrogen peroxide was broken down over a catalyst to produce hot gases (oxygen/water vapor) that drove a turbine to pump fuel. These gases were then mixed with hydrazine/methanol to produce combustion and thrust.
Since the Natter was to be "fired" in a vertical position, Walter developed a version of the HWK 109-509A-2 capable of operating in this position.
In fact , the hydrogen peroxide was conducted into the gas generator by simple gravity and Walter modified the position of this generator giving life to the HWK 109-509E version.
The propulsion offered for the production model Ba-349B was a dedicated version of the Walter HWK 109-509C-1 rocket engine which featured separate combustion chambers for take-off (1700 kg thrust) and cruise (300 kg thrust) and which powered the Me-163C and then the Me-263, improved

versions of the Me-163B.

- The liftoff took place automatically from a vertical ramp about ten meters high under the thrust of the Walter rocket engine and four Schmidding 533 powder boosters of 1000 kgp each for 12 seconds.

The acceleration was strong enough to threaten the pilot with blackout, and the autopilot was also used to steer the plane onto the correct trajectory while the pilot regained consciousness.
After one or two minutes of rocket engine operation, the craft reached an altitude of 12,000 meters.

- The pilot then switched to manual controls and engaged the Natter in level flight at a speed of 990 km/h.

It then dived into enemy formations and destroyed as many aircraft as it could with its 24-48 55 mm R4M rockets (or 73 mm Hs 217 rockets) housed in the nose.
After slowing down to about 250 km/h, the nose of the plane was lowered and the pilot parachuted out: the rear part was also recovered with the parachute so as to be able to reuse the most precious part of the machine: the Walter rocket engine, the whole thing took 3 or 4 minutes.
The wind tunnel models, which had been built at the beginning of the program, were shipped elsewhere for testing and results returned to Bachem designers indicated that it would be "satisfactory" at speeds below 1,100 km/h: full-scale models were then completed and flight testing began in November 1944.
Initial versions did not include any engines, and were towed into the air by a Heinkel He 111 bomber for gliding tests: further launch tests And of the pilot automatic they came carried out with solid-propellant engines .

- They all had positive results, but it appeared obvious That Not would be state possible reuse the engine; the landing speed was simply too high.

Construction of production models of the Ba 349A was already underway started in October, And fifteen Of they came launched in the next few months.

- The Bachem "Natter" represented the world's first manned rocket launch.

Each launch resulted in a slight modification of the design, and these were eventually collected in the definitive production version, the Ba 349B which began testing in January.
U.S. forces seized the Waldsee factory in April, but some Bachem staff managed to escape. carrying with himself the ten remaining aircraft from the series B: But the Americans soon managed to capture them, and six of the ten aircraft were set on fire.

- By February 1945, the SS determined that the program was not progressing fast enough, and ordered an operational launch by the end of the month.

The first and only time That the plane was tested in this way it was The 28 February, when Lothar Sieber flew a Ba 349A, which was launched from the military training area near Stetten

am kalten Markt.
At first, everything seemed to be going well. as expected, but to 500 meters of share there canopy came off: the aircraft, having turned on its back, first rose to 1,500 meters, and then fell to the ground. Sieber died in the accident, and the cause was never identified: it was suspected that the canopy had not been properly secured before the launch.
Some sources claim that a Natter task force was set up by volunteers in Kirchheim unter Teck, but they failed to carry out any operations: however, there is no evidence for this version, which seems rather far-fetched.
In the Hasenholz forest near Kirchheim unter Teck there were three launch sites for the Bachem Ba 349 and they are all that remain of an active launch site built in 1945.

- The Three ramps Of launch I am arranged to form of an equilateral triangle, whose sides point towards the east and towards south: the distance Between the ramps is approximately of 50 meters.

The circular platforms on which the Bachem Ba 349s and their launch towers once stood still exist today: in the centre of each of them there is a square hole about 50 centimetres deep, which served as a foundation. for the launch pad. Next to each hole is a ramp, cut at ground level, which probably once served as a connecting pit. The launch pads of the Natter a Kirchheim (Teck) they could be the only those remaining in areas still accessible to the public.
The first test site for the Natter in Baden-Württemberg near Stetten am Kalten Markt is a military area still in use, and therefore, not It is accessible to tourists.

Technical features

- Length: 6.02 meters
- Opening wing: 3.60 meters
- Height: 2.25 meters
- Surface wing: 2.75 m²
- Weight empty: 880 kg
- Weight max to the takeoff: 2,232 kg
- Propulsion: Walter HWK 109-509A-2 engine with 4 solid-fuel booster rockets
- Thrust:16.7 kN (1,700 kg)
- Speed max: 1,000 km/h (621 mph) at 5,000 meters
- Cruising speed: 800 km/h (497 mph)
- Tangency: 12,000 meters (39,370 feet)
- Rate of climb: 190 m/s (37,000 ft/min)
- Climb time: 62 seconds at 12 km
- Vertical launch: 4 or 2 Schmidding SG 34 monobloc powder rocket motors
- Missiles: 24 x 73 mm Föhn Hs 217 rockets or 33 x 55 mm R4M rockets weighing 3.5 kg each and with a maximum velocity of 525 metres per second, or, optionally, two 30 mm MK 108 cannons each supplied with 30 rounds.

R4M rockets

The R4M was developed to solve the problem of the increasing weight of anti-bomber weapons carried by Luftwaffe fighters.
Their design began with the 20 mm MG 151/20 cannon, which however required an average of 20 shots to shoot down a Boeing B-17 Flying Fortress.
The 20 mm guns were replaced, or supplemented, with 30 mm MK 108 guns, which could down a bomber with one to three hits: however, the MK 108 was heavier and the bulky ammunition made it difficult to carry enough rounds for two or more "passes".
Worse still, the MK 108's low muzzle velocity meant a short range, forcing fighters to get into range of enemy machine guns in order to score hits.

- The more powerful MK 103 had a higher muzzle velocity and longer range, at the cost of much greater weight and size.

The solution was to replace the cannon with a small solid-fuel rocket, carrying a warhead similar to that of the cannon shell. Although each rocket was heavier than the corresponding shell fired by the cannon, the lack of a cannon considerably reduced the overall weight.

- The difference in weight was so marked that even larger rockets would have been lighter than the guns they replaced, and would have performed better, too.

The anti-aircraft version of the R4M used a 55 mm wide warhead loaded with a whopping 520 g of hexogen, ensuring almost one kill for every rocket that hit it.
Each R4M weighed 3.5 kg and carried enough fuel to be

launched from 1,000 metres, beyond the range of the bombers' defensive guns.
The rocket's skeleton consisted of a simple steel tube with fins at the tail for stabilization.
A battery normally consisted of two groups of 12 rockets and if all 24 were fired simultaneously they could cover an area of between 15 and 30 metres at 1,000 metres away, dense enough to be certain of hitting the target.

- The R4Ms were normally fired in four salvos of six missiles at 0.07 second intervals from a range of 600 metres.

Two types of warhead were available for the R4M, the classic PB-3 with a 0.4 kg charge for anti-aircraft use and a larger shaped charge, similar in construction to the Panzerschreck, the Panzerblitz II (PB-2), for anti-tank use.
By April 1945, Me 262 pilots equipped with R4Ms claimed to have shot down thirty B-17s with the loss of three aircraft: the Luftwaffe noted that the R4M rockets had a similar flight trajectory to the MK 108 30 mm cannon shells, and therefore the standard Revi 16B reflecting sight could be used effectively.

The R4M consisted of three parts:

- The warhead with explosive charge.
  The R4M had a Rheinmetall-Borsig explosive charge of the AzRz 2 type with a detonator composed of 85% hydrazoic acid and 15% styphnic acid, an 8 gr booster charge (Zdlg 34 NP), composed of 90% PETN and 10% wax, and a main charge of 400 gr of HTA 41: 45% trinitrotoluene, 40% hexogen and 15% aluminium powder.
  HTA 41 was a shock-enhanced explosive gas, specially developed for the R4M at the DWM plant in Lübeck. The

explosive charge was screwed onto the conical head of the thermoformed plate (with a wall thickness of 0.8 mm).

- The rocket engine.
  The rocket engine had a combustion chamber 375 mm long and 45 mm wide and contained 875 g of fuel in the form of powdered rods. After a burn time of 0.8 seconds (about 200 meters in a straight line), the R4M reached its maximum speed of 550 m/s or 2,000 km/h.

- The tail.
  Attached to the end of the rocket engine nozzle were eight spring-loaded "fins," with a thin wire holding them together before the rocket was launched.

Mistel Project

The Mistel series of composite aircraft is undoubtedly one of the strangest concepts to reach operational status with the Luftwaffe. The original concept was proposed to the RLM in 1941 by Siegfried Holzbauer, a Junkers test pilot.

His idea was to use Ju 88 cells filled with explosives, fly them near a target and crash them into the target after the fighter had released.

The fighter pilot would have controlled the "missile" after release by remote control.

The composite aircraft designated Mistel were used by the special unit Kampfgeschwader 200 to bomb specific targets, thanks, therefore, to the unusual combination of two aircraft joined together.

- The idea was for the two components to take off together, then be guided towards the target by the upper unit element, with the pilot releasing the lower aircraft above the target, but continuing to fly it via a remote link until it crashed into the target.

The most commonly used combination involved a fighter aircraft as a carrier to which a Junkers Ju 88 bomber was attached, via a specially designed system of cables and connections, as the lower part, with an explosive-filled warhead in place of the cockpit.

- To be precise, the Mistel 1 had, as the Bf 109, an example of the F-4 version, and as the Ju 88 the night fighter version with 3,800 kg (8,377 lb) of explosives, capable of piercing 8 metres of steel and/or 20 metres of reinforced concrete.

The Focke-Wulf Fw 190 was subsequently chosen as the superior component: thus the Mistel 2 series took shape.
At one point it was thought to use Heinkel He 177 heavy bombers as the lower element, given the uselessness of these aircraft for the Reich: the fighter would take the bomber into a steep dive and release itself from it by electrically detonating explosive ball joints placed on the spars. main ones.
To the hunting they were removed the machine guns mounted on the wings but the fuselage machine guns/cannons were, however, left mounted. The shock fuse was placed in a long trunk, so as to make to progressively explode the shaped charge warhead before the bomber crashed completely into the target.

- The Mistel could touch the 380 km/h.

The unit responsible for using the Mistel was the Kampfgeschwader 200, KG 200-200th Bomber Wing, which employed it for the first time against Allied troops during the battle of Normandy, June 24, 1944: the attack, carried out against vessels anchored between Cherbourg-Octeville and Le Havre, was successful and several ships were sunk.

- A new one was planned for early 1945. massed Mistel attack on power stations near Moscow which, the Germans estimated, supplied power to about 80% of the Soviet war industry: however, a USAAF daylight raid destroyed many Mistels on the ground before they could take off and consequently the mission was cancelled.

A successful attack, however, was on March 6, 1945, when KG 200 used Mistels to destroy two bridges over the Oder River at Göritz, to slow down the Red Army's advance toward Berlin.

- The first Mistel raid took place on 08/03/45 with two aircraft, against the Goritz bridge on the Oder, destroying the bridge: 1 destroyed the anti-aircraft guns while 1 did not function.

- The second raid took place on 31/03/45, where the railway bridge at Steinau was destroyed: the raid forced the Red Army to slow down the assault on Berlin by a few days.

Only two complete examples survive: one at the RAF Museum Midlands, Cosford, Great Britain, the other at the National Museum of the USAF, Dayton, Ohio, USA.

During the war, approximately 250 Mistels were assembled in various configurations.

- In addition to the Ju 88 / Bf 109, bizarre combinations were experimented with such as the Focke-Wulf Ta 154 night fighter with an Fw 190, the Dornier Do 217K bomber with the DFS 228 reconnaissance glider or even projects that remained on paper which foresaw the use of the Messerschmitt Me 262, Junkers Ju 287 or Arado Ar 234 jets.

The device used was a specialized shaped charge weighing 1,800 kg, equipped with a copper or aluminum cap to increase its penetration capacity, estimated at up to 7 meters of reinforced concrete.

Versions

- **Mistletoe Prototype:** prototype compound from a Yes 88 A-4s and a Bf 109 F-4 fighter.
- **Mistletoe 1:** version Of series composed from a Yes 88 A- 4 And a bf 109 F-4, a from the two really employed in operational missions.
- **Mistletoe S1:** version from training of the Mistletoe 1.
- **Mistel 2:** composition between a Ju 88 Gl and a Fw 190 A-8 or F-8 fighter.
- **Mistletoe S2:** version from training of the Mistletoe 2.
- **Mistel 3°:** composition between a Ju 88 A-4 and a Fw 190 A-8 fighter, one of the two actually used in operational missions.
- **Mistel S3A:** training version of the Mistel 3A.
- **Mistletoe 3B:** composition Between a Yes 88 H-4 And an Fw 190 A-8 fighter.
- **Mistletoe 3C:** composition Between a Yes 88 G-10 And an Fw 190 F-8 fighter.
- **Mistletoe 3A:** composition Between a Yes 88 A-4 And a Fw 190 A-8 fighter.
- **Mistel Führungsmaschine:** composition between a Ju 88 A-4/H-4 and a Fw 190 A-8 fighter.
- **Mistel 4:** composition between a Junkers Ju 287 and a Messerschmitt Me 262.
- **Mistletoe 5:** known Also with there designation RLM Junkers Ju 268, composition between an Arado E377 TO And a hunting interceptor Heinkel He162 remained at the planning stage.

Arado E-377

This project was one of the last glide bomb developments presented to the RLM before the end of World War II. Arado, working with Rheinmetall-Borsig, designed a simple glide bomb, which could be powered or unpowered, and carried under the Arado 234 or Heinkel 162.

- The purpose of this flying bomb, which could be guided by remote control or a target guidance system, was to attack targets such as ships or large stationary targets.

The E.377 was all wooden in construction with the fuselage circular in cross-section.

- Mounted in the nose was 2,000 kg (4,408 lb) of Trialen 105, a high explosive particularly suited to ship attacks.

Additionally, 500 kg (1,202 lb) of an incendiary liquid was stored in the rear fuselage, which also served as ballast, to counterbalance the front.

- A standard SC 1800 bomb could also be installed in the forward fuselage of the E.377 in place of the Trialen 105.

The wings were tapered and also served as auxiliary fuel tanks for the parent aircraft: fuel was extracted from the E.377's tanks by means of jet pressure driving a compressor in the parent aircraft's powerplant.
The tail unit was symmetrical top and bottom with a horizontal tail mounted on the upper half of the fin.
Take-off was accomplished using a landing gear similar to the one Rheinmetall-Borsig had designed for the Arado 234A.

- Since the Arado E.377 was heavier, an extra set of wheels was added to the new landing gear: once the aircraft reached take-off speed, the landing gear was released and slowed down with a parachute and rockets.

Once at the target, the E.377 was released via explosive bolts and then directed towards the target via a control device, or, it could simply be set to glide straight after separation.

Heinkell He 162 with E.377 glide bomb.

- There was also a version with two BMW 003 jet engines for use with the Heinkel 162, as the single jet engine of the He 162 would not have been powerful enough to carry the E.377.

This version was known as the E.377A and was similar in all other respects to the E.377.
A piloted version, to be a suicide weapon, was also planned, but was cancelled before the end of the war.

- The E.377 was, however, never built due to the end of the war.

Technical Features E.377

- Wingspan: 12.2 meters
- Length: 10.9 meters
- Height: 1.4 meters
- Wing area: 27 ^{2}
- Length: 7.65 meters
- Maximum weight: 10,400 kg
- Maximum speed: 720 km/h
- Autonomy: 2,000 km

www.ingramcontent.com/pod-product-compliance
Lightning Source LLC
LaVergne TN
LVHW010454160826
845677LV00012B/2477

* 9 7 8 2 3 7 2 9 7 5 4 2 1 *